food a nutrition

Date:

Breakfast.

Snack. . .

Lunch. . . .

Snack. . .

Dinner. . .

Dessert. . .

Water

Supplements

I believe in me

fitness

Date:

Exercise	Set	Wt	Comments

Cardio	Time	Speed	Distance	Level	Pulse	Calories

food and nutrition

Date:

Breakfast.	
Snack. . .	
Lunch. . . .	
Snack. . .	
Dinner. . .	
Dessert. . .	

Water ♥

Supplements

I believe in me

fitness

Date:

Exercise	Set	Wt	Comments

Cardio	Time	Speed	Distance	Level	Pulse	Calories

food and nutrition

Date:

Breakfast.

Snack. . .

Lunch. . . .

Snack. . .

Dinner. . .

Dessert. . .

Water ♥

Supplements

I believe in me

fitness

Date:

Exercise	Set	Wt	Comments

Cardio	Time	Speed	Distance	Level	Pulse	Calories

food and nutrition

Date:

Breakfast.	
Snack...	
Lunch....	
Snack...	
Dinner...	
Dessert...	

Water ♥

Supplements

I believe in me

Fitness

Date:

Exercise	Set	Wt	Comments

Cardio	Time	Speed	Distance	Level	Pulse	Calories

food and nutrition

Date:

Breakfast.

Snack. . .

Lunch. . . .

Snack. . .

Dinner. . .

Dessert. . .

Water ♥

Supplements

I believe in me

fitness

Date:

Exercise	Set	Wt	Comments

Cardio	Time	Speed	Distance	Level	Pulse	Calories

food and nutrition

Date:

Breakfast.

Snack. . .

Lunch. . . .

Snack. . .

Dinner. . .

Dessert. . .

Water ♥

Supplements

I believe in me

fitness

Date:

Exercise	Set	Wt	Comments

Cardio	Time	Speed	Distance	Level	Pulse	Calories

food and nutrition

Date:

Breakfast.

Snack. . .

Lunch. . . .

Snack. . .

Dinner. . .

Dessert. . .

Water ♥

Supplements

I believe in me

fitness

Date:

Exercise	Set	Wt	Comments

Cardio	Time	Speed	Distance	Level	Pulse	Calories

food and nutrition

Date:

Breakfast.

Snack. . .

Lunch. . . .

Snack. . .

Dinner. . .

Dessert. . .

Water ♥

Supplements

I believe in me

Fitness

Date:

Exercise	Set	Wt	Comments

Cardio	Time	Speed	Distance	Level	Pulse	Calories

food and nutrition

Date:

Breakfast.

Snack. . .

Lunch. . . .

Snack. . .

Dinner. . .

Dessert. . .

Water ♥

Supplements

I believe in me

fitness

Date:

Exercise	Set	Wt	Comments

Cardio	Time	Speed	Distance	Level	Pulse	Calories

food and nutrition

Date: _____

Breakfast.	
Snack. . .	
Lunch. . . .	
Snack. . .	
Dinner. . .	
Dessert. . .	

Water ♥

Supplements

I believe in me

Fitness

Date:

Exercise	Set	Wt	Comments			

Cardio	Time	Speed	Distance	Level	Pulse	Calories

food and nutrition

Date:

Breakfast.

Snack. . .

Lunch. . . .

Snack. . .

Dinner. . .

Dessert. . .

Water 🖤

Supplements

I believe in me

fitness

Date:

Exercise	Set	Wt	Comments

Cardio	Time	Speed	Distance	Level	Pulse	Calories

food and nutrition

Date:

Breakfast.

Snack...

Lunch....

Snack...

Dinner...

Dessert...

Water ♥

Supplements

I believe in me

Fitness

Date:

Exercise	Set	Wt	Comments

Cardio	Time	Speed	Distance	Level	Pulse	Calories

food and nutrition

Date:

Breakfast.	
Snack. . .	
Lunch. . . .	
Snack. . .	
Dinner. . .	
Dessert. . .	

Water ♥

Supplements

I believe in me

Fitness

Date:

Exercise	Set	Wt	Comments

Cardio	Time	Speed	Distance	Level	Pulse	Calories

food and nutrition

Date:

Breakfast.	
Snack. . .	
Lunch. . . .	
Snack. . .	
Dinner. . .	
Dessert. . .	

Water ♥

Supplements

I believe in me

fitness

Date:

Exercise	Set	Wt	Comments			
----------	-----	----	----------			
Cardio	Time	Speed	Distance	Level	Pulse	Calories

food and nutrition

Date:

Breakfast.	
Snack. . .	
Lunch. . . .	
Snack. . .	
Dinner. . .	
Dessert. . .	

Water ♥

Supplements

I believe in me

Fitness

Date:

Exercise	Set	Wt	Comments

Cardio	Time	Speed	Distance	Level	Pulse	Calories

food and nutrition

Date:

Breakfast.	
Snack. . .	
Lunch. . . .	
Snack. . .	
Dinner. . .	
Dessert. . .	

Water ♥

Supplements

I believe in me

fitness

Date:

Exercise	Set	Wt	Comments			
Cardio	Time	Speed	Distance	Level	Pulse	Calories

food and nutrition

Date:

Breakfast.

Snack. . .

Lunch. . . .

Snack. . .

Dinner. . .

Dessert. . .

Water ♥

Supplements

I believe in me

fitness

Date:

Exercise	Set	Wt	Comments			

Cardio	Time	Speed	Distance	Level	Pulse	Calories

food and nutrition

Date:

Breakfast.

Snack. . .

Lunch. . . .

Snack. . .

Dinner. . .

Dessert. . .

Water 💜

Supplements

I believe in me

fitness

Date:

Exercise	Set	Wt	Comments			

Cardio	Time	Speed	Distance	Level	Pulse	Calories

food and nutrition

Date:

Breakfast.

Snack. . .

Lunch. . . .

Snack. . .

Dinner. . .

Dessert. . .

Water ♥

Supplements

I believe in me

fitness

Date:

Exercise	Set	Wt	Comments			

Cardio	Time	Speed	Distance	Level	Pulse	Calories

food and nutrition

Date:

Breakfast.

Snack. . .

Lunch. . . .

Snack. . .

Dinner. . .

Dessert. . .

Water ♥

Supplements

I believe in me

fitness

Date:

Exercise	Set	Wt	Comments			

Cardio	Time	Speed	Distance	Level	Pulse	Calories

food and nutrition

Date:

Breakfast.

Snack. . .

Lunch. . . .

Snack. . .

Dinner. . .

Dessert. . .

Water ♥

Supplements

I believe in me

fitness

Date:

Exercise	Set	Wt	Comments			

Cardio	Time	Speed	Distance	Level	Pulse	Calories

food and nutrition

Date: _____

Breakfast.

Snack. . .

Lunch. . . .

Snack. . .

Dinner. . .

Dessert. . .

Water ♥

Supplements

I believe in me

fitness

Date:

Exercise	Set	Wt	Comments

Cardio	Time	Speed	Distance	Level	Pulse	Calories

food and nutrition

Date:

Breakfast.	
Snack. . .	
Lunch. . . .	
Snack. . .	
Dinner. . .	
Dessert. . .	

Water ♥

Supplements

I believe in me

fitness

Date:

Exercise	Set	Wt	Comments			

Cardio	Time	Speed	Distance	Level	Pulse	Calories

food and nutrition

Date:

Breakfast.

Snack. . .

Lunch. . . .

Snack. . .

Dinner. . .

Dessert. . .

Water ♥

Supplements

I believe in me

fitness

Date:

Exercise	Set	Wt	Comments			

Cardio	Time	Speed	Distance	Level	Pulse	Calories

food and nutrition

Date:

Breakfast.	
Snack. . .	
Lunch. . . .	
Snack. . .	
Dinner. . .	
Dessert. . .	

Water ♥

Supplements

I believe in me

fitness

Date:

Exercise	Set	Wt	Comments			

Cardio	Time	Speed	Distance	Level	Pulse	Calories

food and nutrition

Date:

Breakfast.	
Snack. . .	
Lunch. . . .	
Snack. . .	
Dinner. . .	
Dessert. . .	

Water ♥

Supplements

I believe in me

Fitness

Date:

Exercise	Set	Wt	Comments

Cardio	Time	Speed	Distance	Level	Pulse	Calories

food and nutrition

Date:

Breakfast.

Snack. . .

Lunch. . . .

Snack. . .

Dinner. . .

Dessert. . .

Water ♥

Supplements

I believe in me

fitness

Date:

Exercise	Set	Wt	Comments

Cardio	Time	Speed	Distance	Level	Pulse	Calories

food and nutrition

Date:

Breakfast.

Snack. . .

Lunch. . . .

Snack. . .

Dinner. . .

Dessert. . .

Water ♥

Supplements

I believe in me

Fitness

Date:

Exercise	Set	Wt	Comments

Cardio	Time	Speed	Distance	Level	Pulse	Calories

food and nutrition

Date:

Breakfast.	
Snack. . .	
Lunch. . . .	
Snack. . .	
Dinner. . .	
Dessert. . .	

Water ♥

Supplements

I believe in me

fitness

Date:

Exercise	Set	Wt	Comments

Cardio	Time	Speed	Distance	Level	Pulse	Calories

food and nutrition

Date:

Breakfast.	
Snack. . .	
Lunch. . . .	
Snack. . .	
Dinner. . .	
Dessert. . .	

Water ♥

Supplements

I believe in me

fitness

Date:

Exercise	Set	Wt	Comments			
Cardio	Time	Speed	Distance	Level	Pulse	Calories

food and nutrition

Date:

Breakfast.

Snack. . .

Lunch. . . .

Snack. . .

Dinner. . .

Dessert. . .

Water ♥

Supplements

I believe in me

fitness

Date:

Exercise	Set	Wt	Comments			

Cardio	Time	Speed	Distance	Level	Pulse	Calories

food and nutrition

Date:

Breakfast.	
Snack. . .	
Lunch. . . .	
Snack. . .	
Dinner. . .	
Dessert. . .	

Water ♥

Supplements

I believe in me

fitness

Date:

Exercise	Set	Wt	Comments			

Cardio	Time	Speed	Distance	Level	Pulse	Calories

food and nutrition

Date:

Breakfast.

Snack. . .

Lunch. . . .

Snack. . .

Dinner. . .

Dessert. . .

Water ♥

Supplements

I believe in me

fitness

Date:

Exercise	Set	Wt	Comments

Cardio	Time	Speed	Distance	Level	Pulse	Calories

food and nutrition

Date:

Breakfast.

Snack. . .

Lunch. . . .

Snack. . .

Dinner. . .

Dessert. . .

Water

Supplements

I believe in me

fitness

Date:

Exercise	Set	Wt	Comments

Cardio	Time	Speed	Distance	Level	Pulse	Calories

food and nutrition

Date:

Breakfast.	
Snack. . .	
Lunch. . . .	
Snack. . .	
Dinner. . .	
Dessert. . .	

Water ♥

Supplements

I believe in me

Fitness

Date:

Exercise	Set	Wt	Comments		

Cardio	Time	Speed	Distance	Level	Pulse	Calories

food and nutrition

Date:

Breakfast.

Snack. . .

Lunch. . . .

Snack. . .

Dinner. . .

Dessert. . .

Water ♥

Supplements

I believe in me

Fitness

Date:

Exercise	Set	Wt	Comments			

Cardio	Time	Speed	Distance	Level	Pulse	Calories

food and nutrition

Date:

Breakfast.

Snack. . .

Lunch. . . .

Snack. . .

Dinner. . .

Dessert. . .

Water ♥

Supplements

I believe in me

fitness

Date:

Exercise	Set	Wt	Comments

Cardio	Time	Speed	Distance	Level	Pulse	Calories

food and nutrition

Date:

Breakfast.

Snack. . .

Lunch. . . .

Snack. . .

Dinner. . .

Dessert. . .

Water ♥

Supplements

I believe in me

Fitness

Date:

Exercise	Set	Wt	Comments

Cardio	Time	Speed	Distance	Level	Pulse	Calories

food and nutrition

Date:

Breakfast.

Snack. . .

Lunch. . . .

Snack. . .

Dinner. . .

Dessert. . .

Water ♥

Supplements

I believe in me

Fitness

Date:

Exercise	Set	Wt	Comments

Cardio	Time	Speed	Distance	Level	Pulse	Calories

food and nutrition

Date:

Breakfast.

Snack...

Lunch....

Snack...

Dinner...

Dessert...

Water ♥

Supplements

I believe in me

Fitness

Date:

Exercise	Set	Wt	Comments

Cardio	Time	Speed	Distance	Level	Pulse	Calories

food and nutrition

Date:

Breakfast.

Snack. . .

Lunch. . . .

Snack. . .

Dinner. . .

Dessert. . .

Water ♥

Supplements

I believe in me

fitness

Date:

Exercise	Set	Wt	Comments

Cardio	Time	Speed	Distance	Level	Pulse	Calories

food and nutrition

Date:

Breakfast.

Snack. . .

Lunch. . . .

Snack. . .

Dinner. . .

Dessert. . .

Water ♥

Supplements

I believe in me

fitness

Date:

Exercise	Set	Wt	Comments

Cardio	Time	Speed	Distance	Level	Pulse	Calories

food and nutrition

Date:

Breakfast.

Snack. . .

Lunch. . . .

Snack. . .

Dinner. . .

Dessert. . .

Water ♥

Supplements

I believe in me

fitness

Date:

Exercise	Set	Wt	Comments

Cardio	Time	Speed	Distance	Level	Pulse	Calories

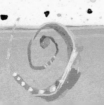

food and nutrition

Date:

Breakfast.	
Snack. . .	
Lunch. . . .	
Snack. . .	
Dinner. . .	
Dessert. . .	

Water ♥

Supplements

I believe in me

fitness

Date:

Exercise	Set	Wt	Comments			

Cardio	Time	Speed	Distance	Level	Pulse	Calories

food and nutrition

Date:

Breakfast.

Snack. . .

Lunch. . . .

Snack. . .

Dinner. . .

Dessert. . .

Water ♥

Supplements

I believe in me

fitness

Date:

Exercise	Set	Wt	Comments

Cardio	Time	Speed	Distance	Level	Pulse	Calories

food and nutrition

Date:

Breakfast.

Snack. . .

Lunch. . . .

Snack. . .

Dinner. . .

Dessert. . .

Water ♥

Supplements

I believe in me

fitness

Date:

Exercise	Set	Wt	Comments			

Cardio	Time	Speed	Distance	Level	Pulse	Calories

food and nutrition

Date:

Breakfast.	
Snack. . .	
Lunch. . . .	
Snack. . .	
Dinner. . .	
Dessert. . .	

Water ♥

Supplements

I believe in me

fitness

Date:

Exercise	Set	Wt	Comments

Cardio	Time	Speed	Distance	Level	Pulse	Calories

food and nutrition

Date:

Breakfast.	
Snack. . .	
Lunch. . . .	
Snack. . .	
Dinner. . .	
Dessert. . .	

Water ♥

Supplements

I believe in me

fitness

Date:

Exercise	Set	Wt	Comments			

Cardio	Time	Speed	Distance	Level	Pulse	Calories

food and nutrition

Date:

Breakfast.

Snack. . .

Lunch. . . .

Snack. . .

Dinner. . .

Dessert. . .

Water ♥

Supplements

I believe in me

fitness

Date:

Exercise	Set	Wt	Comments

Cardio	Time	Speed	Distance	Level	Pulse	Calories

food and nutrition

Date:

Breakfast.

Snack. . .

Lunch. . . .

Snack. . .

Dinner. . .

Dessert. . .

Water ♥

Supplements

I believe in me

fitness

Date:

Exercise	Set	Wt	Comments

Cardio	Time	Speed	Distance	Level	Pulse	Calories

food and nutrition

Date:

Breakfast.	
Snack. . .	
Lunch. . . .	
Snack. . .	
Dinner. . .	
Dessert. . .	

Water ♥

Supplements

I believe in me

fitness

Date:

Exercise	Set	Wt	Comments

Cardio	Time	Speed	Distance	Level	Pulse	Calories

food and nutrition

Date:

Breakfast.

Snack. . .

Lunch. . . .

Snack. . .

Dinner. . .

Dessert. . .

Water ♥

Supplements

I believe in me

fitness

Date:

Exercise	Set	Wt	Comments

Cardio	Time	Speed	Distance	Level	Pulse	Calories

food and nutrition

Date:

Breakfast.	
Snack. . .	
Lunch. . . .	
Snack. . .	
Dinner. . .	
Dessert. . .	

Water ♥

Supplements

I believe in me

fitness

Date:

Exercise	Set	Wt	Comments

Cardio	Time	Speed	Distance	Level	Pulse	Calories

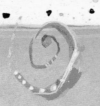

food and nutrition

Date:

Breakfast.

Snack. . .

Lunch. . . .

Snack. . .

Dinner. . .

Dessert. . .

Water ♥

Supplements

I believe in me

fitness

Date:

Exercise	Set	Wt	Comments

Cardio	Time	Speed	Distance	Level	Pulse	Calories

food and nutrition

Date:

Breakfast.	
Snack. . .	
Lunch. . . .	
Snack. . .	
Dinner. . .	
Dessert. . .	

Water ♥

Supplements

I believe in me

fitness

Date:

Exercise	Set	Wt	Comments

Cardio	Time	Speed	Distance	Level	Pulse	Calories

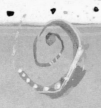

food and nutrition

Date:

Breakfast.

Snack. . .

Lunch. . . .

Snack. . .

Dinner. . .

Dessert. . .

Water ♥

Supplements

I believe in me

Fitness

Date:

Exercise	Set	Wt	Comments			

Cardio	Time	Speed	Distance	Level	Pulse	Calories

food and nutrition

Date:

Breakfast.

Snack. . .

Lunch. . . .

Snack. . .

Dinner. . .

Dessert. . .

Water ♥

Supplements

I believe in me

fitness

Date:

Exercise	Set	Wt	Comments			

Cardio	Time	Speed	Distance	Level	Pulse	Calories

food and nutrition

Date:

Breakfast.

Snack . . .

Lunch . . . .

Snack . . .

Dinner . . .

Dessert . . .

Water ♥

Supplements

I believe in me

Fitness

Date:

Exercise	Set	Wt	Comments			
Cardio	Time	Speed	Distance	Level	Pulse	Calories

food and nutrition

Date:

Breakfast.

Snack. . .

Lunch. . . .

Snack. . .

Dinner. . .

Dessert. . .

Water ♥

Supplements

I believe in me

Fitness

Date:

Exercise	Set	Wt	Comments

Cardio	Time	Speed	Distance	Level	Pulse	Calories

food and nutrition

Date:

Breakfast.

Snack. . .

Lunch. . . .

Snack. . .

Dinner. . .

Dessert. . .

Water ♥

Supplements

I believe in me

fitness

Date:

Exercise	Set	Wt	Comments

Cardio	Time	Speed	Distance	Level	Pulse	Calories

food and nutrition

Date:

Breakfast.

Snack. . .

Lunch. . . .

Snack. . .

Dinner. . .

Dessert. . .

Water 🧡

Supplements

I believe in me

fitness

Date:

Exercise	Set	Wt	Comments

Cardio	Time	Speed	Distance	Level	Pulse	Calories

food and nutrition

Date:

Breakfast.

Snack. . .

Lunch. . . .

Snack. . .

Dinner. . .

Dessert. . .

Water ♥

Supplements

I believe in me

fitness

Date:

Exercise	Set	Wt	Comments

Cardio	Time	Speed	Distance	Level	Pulse	Calories

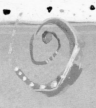

food and nutrition

Date:

Breakfast.

Snack. . .

Lunch. . . .

Snack. . .

Dinner. . .

Dessert. . .

Water ♥

Supplements

I believe in me

fitness

Date:

Exercise	Set	Wt	Comments

Cardio	Time	Speed	Distance	Level	Pulse	Calories

food and nutrition

Date:

Breakfast.

Snack. . .

Lunch. . . .

Snack. . .

Dinner. . .

Dessert. . .

Water ♥

Supplements

I believe in me

fitness

Date:

Exercise	Set	Wt	Comments

Cardio	Time	Speed	Distance	Level	Pulse	Calories

food and nutrition

Date:

Breakfast.

Snack. . .

Lunch. . . .

Snack. . .

Dinner. . .

Dessert. . .

Water ♥

Supplements

I believe in me

fitness

Date:

Exercise	Set	Wt	Comments			

Cardio	Time	Speed	Distance	Level	Pulse	Calories

food and nutrition

Date:

Breakfast.

Snack. . .

Lunch. . . .

Snack. . .

Dinner. . .

Dessert. . .

Water ♥

Supplements

I believe in me

fitness

Date:

Exercise	Set	Wt	Comments			

Cardio	Time	Speed	Distance	Level	Pulse	Calories

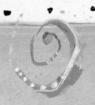